DC SUPER HEROES

MONSTER JOKES

BY MICHAEL DAHL
& DONALD LEMKE

STONE ARCH BOOKS
a capstone imprint

Published by Capstone Young Readers in 2018
A Capstone Imprint
1710 Roe Crest Drive
North Mankato, Minnesota 56003
www.capstonepub.com

STAR39968

Cataloging-in-Publication Data is available on the
Library of Congress website.

ISBN: 978-1-4965-5763-6 (library hardcover)
ISBN: 978-1-4965-5767-4 (eBook)

Summary: What hand should Superman use to pet Titano? Someone
else's! This official DC Comics joke book, featuring Superman, Batman,
Wonder Woman, and other DC Super Heroes, is packed with dozens of
laugh-out-loud jokes about MONSTERS.

Designer: Brann Garvey

Printed in China.
010734S18

Why did Aquaman sleep with a night-light?
He was afraid of sea monsters under his bed!

What is the scariest place for Aquaman to swim?
Lake Eerie.

What is the second scariest place for Aquaman to swim?
The Dead Sea.

What did Aqualad say when he
first saw an ocean monster?

"See? Serpent!"

What is Aquaman's secret weapon
for defeating sea monsters?

His mussels.

What is a
sea monster's
favorite dish?

**Fish and
ships!**

What did Lex Luthor get when he crossed a skunk with a giant?

A big stink!

What happened when a monster ate Lex Luthor's uranium?

He got atomic-ache!

What did Lex Luthor get when he crossed
Comet the Super-Horse with a monster?
A night-mare.

What did Lex Luthor create when
he combined a cocker spaniel,
a poodle, and a ghost?
A cocker-poodle-boo!

I have a
hair-raising
story about
a monster . . .

**Well,
don't tell
Lex Luthor!**

What do you call Krypto the Super-Dog when he sees a monster?
Super Pet-rified!

Why did Krypto and the werewolf stop fighting?
They were both dog-tired.

How did Krypto lose track of the evil monster?
He was barking up the wrong tree!

What type of Super-Pet is good at catching vampires?
A blood hound.

What do you get when you cross
Supergirl with a ghost?
Super-ghoul!

What did Jimmy Olsen get
when he took a photo of a
two-headed monster?
A double exposure!

What happens when a monster rides
in Wonder Woman's Invisible Jet?
It's a terror-flying experience!

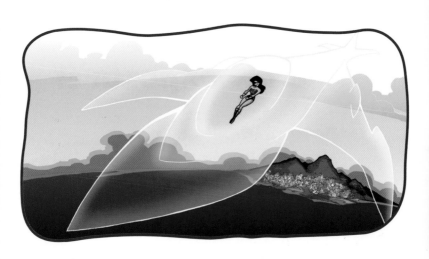

Where do cyclops come from?
Paradise Eye-land.

What is as tall as Giganta but
doesn't weigh anything?
Giganta's shadow!

How can you tell when Green Arrow
is afraid of monsters?
He has a quiver.

Is the Atom ever afraid
of monsters?
Just a tiny bit!

What does Silver Banshee
put on her bagels?
Scream cheese.

What is Silver Banshee's favorite
ice cream topping?
Whipped scream!

What do you call a
Bizarro mummy?
Daddy.

What do you call a
Bizarro vampire?
Alive.

What do you call a
Bizarro werewolf?
A therewolf.

What do you call a Bizarro insect?
An outsect.

Why did Lois Lane choose to write her news story at a cemetery?

Because there are so many plots there!

What happened when the ghost visited the Daily Planet Building?
He turned Perry White!

What is General Zod's favorite musical?
Phantom Zone of the Opera.

What did Bizarro say to his son after he hadn't seen him for a while?
You grew-some.

Where did zombie Bizarro come from?
Crypt-on!

How does Superman keep
zombies from invading the
Fortress of Solitude?

He uses a
dead-bolt lock!

Has Wonder Woman ever seen
the Abominable Snowman?
Not Yeti!

What side of Titano has
the most hair?
The outside.

Why can't the cyclops see anymore?
**Wonder Woman
caught his eye.**

What does Titano call an
exploding monkey?
A ba-boom!

What happens when
Batman gets scared?
**He gets
Bruce-bumps.**

What happened when
the Joker saw a ghost?
He got scared silly!

What road in Gotham City has the
most ghosts haunting it?
A dead end.

What did Mr. Freeze say when he saw the Abominable Snowman? **"Icy you!"**

What's the difference between Batman
and the Abominable Snowman?

**One likes justice,
and the other
likes just ice.**

What do you get if a huge, hairy
monster steps on Batman and Robin?

Flatman and Ribbon!

Why did Dracula visit the Batcave?

To hang out!

Where does zombie
Batman like to hide?

The Bat-grave.

What do you get when you cross The Flash with a monster?

Scary Allen!

What kind of fur can you
get from Gorilla Grodd?
**As fur away
as possible!**

Which hand should you
use to pet Titano?
Someone else's!

What did Superman say to the giant
ape when it did something wrong?
"Titano-no!"

What does Titano call a
well-balanced meal?
**A hero in
each hand!**

What do you get when you cross
Hal Jordan with a ghost?
Scream Lantern!

What do you get when you cross Hal
Jordan with the Abominable Snowman?
Mean Lantern!

How are Sinestro and
a scaredy-cat alike?

They're both yellow.

What's the safest way to explore a dark, scary cave?

Take a Lantern with you!

What does Glomulus want
to be for Halloween?
A goblin!

How did Zatanna make
the Minotaur fall asleep?
**She turned him into
a bull-dozer!**

What would you call 144
Swamp Things stuffed in a box?
Gross.

How does Scarecrow keep
cool in the summer?
**He uses a
scare-conditioner!**

WHY DIDN'T GRODD EAT THE FLASH?

He hated fast food!

Why did Shazam suspect his father was a vampire?
Because he's a Bat-son!

What did The Flash find between the giant monster's toes?
Slow runners!

What type of truck does
Gorilla Grodd drive?

A monster truck!

What do you call Gorilla Grodd
in a phone booth?

Stuck.

When is a wall like Killer Croc?
When it is scaled.

How does the villain
Scarecrow like his eggs?
Terror-fried!

What's the swamp-dwelling villain
Solomon Grundy's favorite snack?
Marsh-mallows!

What happens when Nightwing sees a zombie?
He gets flight-ened!

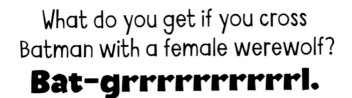
What do you get if you cross
Batman with a female werewolf?

Bat-grrrrrrrrrl.

Why is Killer Croc so good at creeping up on people?
He's a crept-tile.

What did Scarecrow wear to the fancy dinner?
A boo-tie!

Why don't Batman or Dracula have many friends?
They both have bat-breath.

What is Scarecrow's favorite fruit?
Straw-berries.

What do little monsters like
to ride at the amusement park?
The scary-go-round.

What is Scarecrow's favorite color?
Blooooo!

Why does Scarecrow have
good hearing?
**Because he's
so ear-ie.**

Where did baby Scarecrow go
while his parents were at work?
Day-scare!

What does Scarecrow like
to eat for supper?
Spook-etti!

DAILY PLANET DEADLINES!

SUPERMAN BATTLES THE LOCH NESS MONSTER

by Scott Land

CYBORG'S ATTACK

by Ann Droid

BIZARRO EXILED FROM EARTH

by Nada Lowd

KILLER CROC ON THE LOOSE!

by Ali Gader

TITANO CLIMBS DAILY PLANET BUILDING!

By Andover Hand

WHO'S ROBBING GRAVES IN GOTHAM CITY?

by Ivan Alibi

DRACULA STEALS BATMOBILE!

by Grant Otto Theff

BATMAN TURNS INTO WEREWOLF

by Oliver Sudden

What do you call Solomon Grundy
when he uses a phone?
A dead ringer!

Which of Superman's foes is
the easiest to defeat?
Lex Loser!

How is Wonder Woman's
Invisible Jet like a blizzard?
**When you look
outside, there's
sno-wing in sight!**

Where is the Gotham City
cemetery located?
**In the dead center
of town.**

How did the hairdresser beat
The Flash in a race?

She knew a shortcut!

What's black and white
and red all over?

**The Penguin with
a sunburn!**

What happened when Wonder
Woman trapped Cheetah
with her lasso?

**The villain
was knot
happy!**

WHICH WEAPON OF WONDER WOMAN'S DIDN'T DO A VERY GOOD JOB?

Her lasso-so.

53

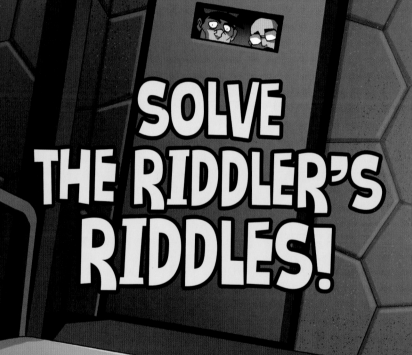

1. What time is it when you see a monster?

2. What room is useless for a ghost?

3. Where does Dracula keep his money?

4. How do you make a witch itch?

5. Why do werewolves have such large families?

6. What do ghosts like for dessert?

ANSWERS:

1. Time to run.
2. A living room.
3. A blood bank.
4. Take away the W.
5. Each has four paws.
6. Ice cream.

HOW TO TELL JOKES!

1. KNOW the joke.
Make sure you remember the whole joke before you tell it. This sounds like a no-brainer, but most of us have known someone who says, "Oh, this is so funny . . ." Then, when they tell the joke, they can't remember the end. And that's the whole point of a joke — its punch line.

2. SPEAK CLEARLY.
Don't mumble; don't speak too fast or too slow. Just speak like you normally do. You don't have to use a different voice or accent or sound like someone else.

3. LOOK at your audience.
Good eye contact with your listeners will grab their attention.

4. DON'T WORRY about gestures or how to stand or sit when you tell your joke. Remember, telling a joke is basically talking.

5. DON'T LAUGH at your own joke.
Yeah, yeah, I know some comedians break up while they're acting in a sketch or telling a story, but the best rule to follow is not to laugh. If you start to laugh, you might lose the rhythm of your joke or keep yourself from telling the joke clearly. Let your audience laugh. That's their job. Your job is to be the funny one.

6. THE PUNCH LINE is the most important part of the joke.

It's the climax, the payoff, the main event. A good joke can sound even better if you pause for just a second or two before you deliver the punch line. That tiny pause will make your audience mentally sit up and hold their breath, eager to hear what's coming next.

7. The SETUP is the second most important part of a joke.

That's basically everything you say before you get to the punch line. And that's why you need to be as clear as you can (see 2) so that when you finally reach the punch line, it makes sense!

8. YOU CAN GET FUNNIER.

It's easy. Watch other comedians. Listen to other people tell a joke or story. Check out a good comedy show or film. You can pick up some skills simply by seeing how others get their comedy across. You will absorb it! And soon it will come naturally.

9. Last, but not least, telling a joke is all about TIMING.

That means not only getting the biggest impact for your joke, waiting for the right time, giving that extra pause before the punch line — but it also means knowing when NOT to tell a joke. When you're among friends, you can tell when they'd like to hear something funny. But in an unfamiliar setting, get a "sense of the room" first. Are people having a good time? Or is it a more serious event? A joke has the most funny power when it's told in the right setting.

MICHAEL DAHL

Michael Dahl is the prolific author of the bestselling *Goodnight, Baseball* picture book and more than 200 other books for children and young adults. He has won the AEP Distinguished Achievement Award three times for his nonfiction, a Teacher's Choice award from *Learning* magazine, and a Seal of Excellence from the Creative Child Awards. And he has won awards for his board books for the earliest learners, *Duck Goes Potty* and *Bear Says "Thank You!"* Dahl has written and edited numerous graphic novels for younger readers, authored the Library of Doom adventure series, the Dragonblood books, Trollhunters, and the Hocus Pocus Hotel mystery/comedy series. Dahl has spoken at schools, libraries, and conferences across the US and the UK, including ALA, AASL, IRA, and Renaissance Learning. He currently lives in Minneapolis, Minnesota, in a haunted house.

DONALD LEMKE

Donald Lemke works as a children's book editor. He has written dozens of all-age comics and children's books for Capstone, HarperCollins, Running Press, and more. Donald lives in St. Paul, Minnesota, with his brilliant wife, Amy, two toddling toddlers, and a not-so-golden retriever named Paulie.

JOKE DICTIONARY!

bit (BIT)—a section of a comedy routine

comedian (kuh-MEE-dee-uhn)—an entertainer who makes people laugh

headliner (HED-lye-ner)—the last comedian to perform in a show

improvisation (im-PRAH-vuh-ZAY-shuhn)—a performance that hasn't been planned; "improv" for short

lineup (LINE-uhp)—a list of people who are going to perform in a show

one-liner (WUHN-lye-ner)—a short joke or funny remark

open mike (OH-puhn MIKE)—an event at which anyone can use the microphone to perform for the audience

punch line (PUHNCH line)—the words at the end of a joke that make it funny or surprising

shtick (SHTIK)—a repetitive, comic performance or routine

segue (SEG-way)—a sentence or phrase that leads from one joke or routine to another

stand-up (STAND-uhp)—the type of comedy performed while standing alone on stage

timing (TIME-ing)—the use of rhythm and tempo to make a joke funnier

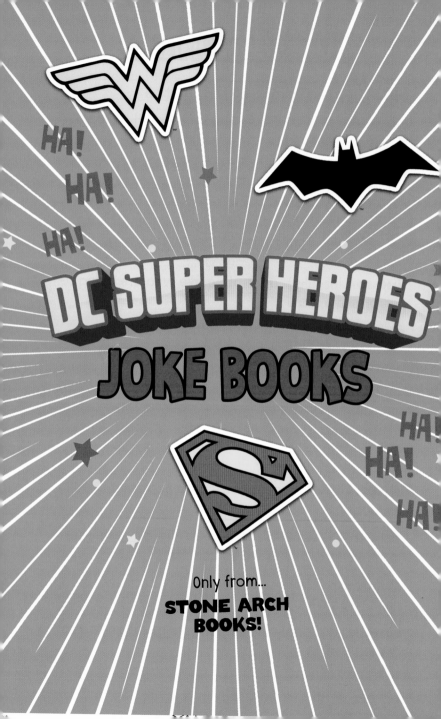

DC SUPER HEROES

JOKE BOOKS

HA!
HA!
HA!

HA!
HA!
HA!

Only from...

**STONE ARCH
BOOKS!**

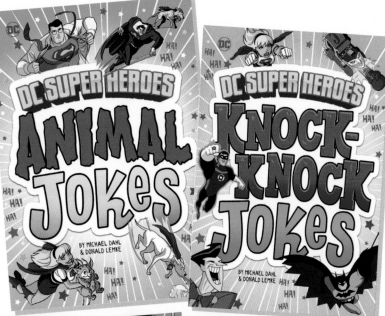

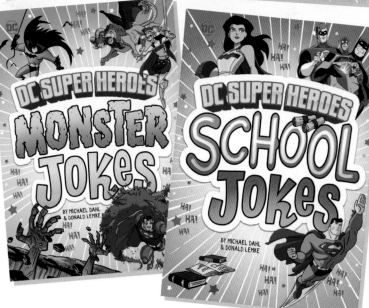